Laugh Lines

A Collection of Silly Poems for Silly Seniors

Maggie Keefe

drawings by Vaughan Duck

First published by Margaret Keefe, 2025

Text & illustration copyright © Margaret Keefe, 2025

Illustrations and design by Vaughan Duck

ISBN : 979-8-9864872-8-1 (Paperback)
ISBN : 979-8-9864872-9-8 (Hardback)

Created by
Humans

For all my senior friends
who are surviving the trials of old age
with the help of optimism, wit, humor
and modern medicine.

Do You Remember?

When candy was a penny
And hitchhiking was a thing.
You learned to write in cursive
And the phone had just one ring.

Before the days of spell check
And apps for everything.

You played outside with other kids

No organized playdates.

Just be home for supper

(And you better not be late).

If you remember all these things

With a longing in your heart.

Then I can say with confidence,

You must be an old fart!

Hip, Hip Horray

Hip hip hooray!
I have a new hip.
The old one was faulty
and caused me to slip.

I hope that the new one
will swivel and twirl.
And allow me to dance
as I did when a girl.

Oh, how freely I moved
back in the day.
Like a tree in the wind,
I would gracefully sway.

I'm hopeful a new hip
will free me of pain.
And allow me to prance,
dance, and frolic again.

But I guess at this age,
I'd be grateful instead,
If this new hip
allows me to get out of bed.

Cursing Machine

He's a grouchy, complaining,

cursing machine.

A grumpy old man

who can be pretty mean.

And if you don't like it,

go spit in your hat.

And don't ever tell him,

"Now, don't be like that."

He's not gonna change.

Not at his age.

He's earned the right

to this grumpy-guy stage.

And he rather enjoys it.

He can speak his mind.

His thoughts and his words

are no longer confined

To what's proper or fitting

or even accepted.

His words may offend.

They are not what's expected.

But he doesn't care.

He's spent his whole life

Toeing the line and saying what's right.

He's enjoying old age

and the freedom it brings

And to not give a damn

what anyone thinks.

His relations may suffer,

and that's fine with him.

The chance of him changing

appears rather slim.

So you better get used
to the grouchy old man.
He won't stop complaining.
I don't think he can.
But look on the bright side:
at age 97,
Soon he'll be doing
his cursing in heaven.

Senior Day at Price Cutter

She counts out her change
in nickels and dimes.
She's not in a hurry;
she takes her sweet time.
You'll just have to wait;
"What was the amount?"
Here come the pennies.
Oh, great! She's lost count.

My ice cream is melting;
my milk has gone sour.
I just hope I leave before closing hour.

NOOO,

here come the coupons!
Most have expired.
She argues each one;
the cashier looks tired.

I could pay it forward
and pick up the tab.
She would put all her loose change
back in her bag.
I smile and offer,
but she gives me a scowl.
"I don't need your charity,"
she says with a growl.

I think there's an opening
in lane number nine.
I hurry on over;
take my place in the line.
He counts out his change
in nickels and dimes.
He's not in a hurry;
he takes his sweet time.

Old Man in a Hat

Old man in a hat
with no need to rush.
He pulls out so slowly.
Does he need a push?

The light has turned green.
Does he need a nudge?
All my honking and yelling
does not make him budge.

He's not being rude.
He just doesn't hear.
Too much Led Zeppelin
has ruined his ears.

His blinker's been on since 1968.
And every ten feet,
he's tapping his brakes.

Leaving the house
instills me with dread.
Most of the drivers
are like walking dead.
Oh, these Florida roads
do fill me with fear.

Old men in hats
are found everywhere.

I am Strong

A soft rain,
The air is damp.
Surrounded by green smells.
Turkey vultures overhead.
Do they sense my weakness?
They are circling.
Getting closer.
I can almost touch them.
Suddenly, they change direction
Chasing a flock of small birds.
I am too strong for them.
Try again when
I am older and weaker.

For now, I am just old.

It's Funny
Because It's True

At 25,

The phone rings at midnight.

Anticipation, eagerness, excitement.

Undoubtedly good news.

What other type of news is there?

An admirer who cannot sleep.
They must confess their undying love!
Passion, urgency, obsession.
A long-lost friend cannot wait to see me.

For I am
irresistible, fascinating, charming.
I am the winner,
Prosperity, affluence, abundance.
Voice filled with expectation.

"HELLO."

Sorry, wrong number...click.

Head hits the pillow, return to dream.
Peaceful, calm, restful.

At 65,

The phone rings at midnight.

Mind reeling, tense, nerves rattled.

Undoubtedly bad news.

What other type of news is there?

Trouble, emergency, crisis.

Heading for a dark place.

Who died?

Voice filled with dread.

Sorry, wrong number...click.

Heart pounding, hands sweating,
blood pressure soaring.
Stress-related illnesses taking hold.
Perhaps another mini-stroke,
Unease, unrest, insomnia.

Aging with Grace

Our story is etched on our skin.
The wrinkles and lines
show where we have been.

Each face is unique
with a tale to tell
Of a life filled with laughter
and heartache, as well.

The happy times
make for smile lines.
And worry furrows our brow.

The Botox injection erases our past.
Our stories, our history, gone in a flash.

Our skin now has nothing
of interest to say,
But we look ten years younger
than we did yesterday.

So bring on the Botox.

Shoot us up, please!

So what if our face
Doesn't move when
we sneeze.

I'm not aging with grace
Without fighting like hell.
There are some stories
Faces don't need to tell.

The Sound of Silence

So peaceful by the pond;
I do not hear a sound.
The sweet, sweet sound of silence,
is so seldom to be found.

No beeping, honking, people talking,
planes or trains or crows a-squawking.
No frogs or peepers, no lawnmowers,
No dogs barking or leaf blowers.

The silence is so lovely,

I think I'll take a nap.

"What's that, you say?"

I can't hear you.

My hearing aid is off.

Where Are My Keys?

Where are my keys?

Must be in my coat.

Where is my coat?

Might be in the car.

Where is my car?

Wait...I don't have a car.

Guess I don't need my keys anymore.

But I could use a ride
if you're going my way.
It's Senior Day at Price Cutter today.
I've got all my coupons;
I'm ready to go.
Wait, where is my wallet?
Must be in my coat.
Where is my coat?
Might be in the car...

Grow Old OR

Your joints get stiffer,
and your bones may get frail.
Your muscles get weaker,
and you move like a snail.

You lose a few inches;
you gain a few pounds.
You hum to yourself
and make groaning sounds.

Your bladder starts leaking;
your hair starts to thin.
The ladies may notice
some fur on their chin.

This may sound unpleasant
and not worth engaging,
But I have found an upside
to all this aging.

There are senior discounts
and Meals on Wheels.
You can wear comfy shoes
and forget about heels.

There's more time for family
and to pursue your ambition.
You can write silly poems
or simply go fishin'.

You tend to find comfort
in being yourself.
And the things that you value
are people, not wealth.

Old age is a privilege,
and let it be said:
Our options are few:
grow old or drop dead.

JELLO

There's cherry and lemon,
raspberry, and lime.
And a serving won't cost
much more than a dime.
You can mold it or fold it
or make a parfait.
It's easy to chew.
What more can I say?

A dollop of Cool Whip
sure makes it look great
As it wiggles and jiggles
and slides off your plate.

Right off the dish
and onto the floor.
It bounces and shimmies
its way out the door.

And out to the street,

no longer in sight.

I think it sprung wings

and took off in flight.

Perhaps I should try

a tasty fruit cup.

It's not all that tasty,

but it does fill me up.

Or a cookie, or brownie,

or a nice slice of cake.

A dessert that stays put

and won't wander away,

Since I can't seem to get

this darn Jello to stay!

Bucket List

Her family and friends think
she must be insane.
87 years old and up in a small plane!

It's a bucket list item
she intends to complete:
To jump out of this plane
and land on her feet.

Suddenly, she considers
the chute might get stuck.
This could be the moment
she runs out of luck.

So what if she does?

She'll go out in style.

(Though she was kind of hoping

to be around for a while.)

Her name in the papers, her face on TV.

For all of her friends and family to see.

They'll all praise her courage.

"Wow, what a dame!"

But she won't be around

to enjoy all the fame.

Maybe instead,
she'll take on item nine
And finish an entire bottle of wine.

She crossed this one off
her list twice last week,
But never a red,
which would be unique.

She's 87 years old
and feeling quite merry.
Maybe tomorrow
it won't seem so scary.

Old Souls

I did not see it coming.
My back was to the sun.
It snuck up on me quickly.
I was having too much fun.

It tapped me on the shoulder,
It kicked me in the knee.
Old age will sneak up on you,
Slipping in silently.

You do your best to keep it out
With supplements and such,
But collagen and fish oil
Can only do so much.

So keep your eye out, deary,
It will take you by surprise.
It's right around the corner
And will poke you in the eyes.

Next thing you know,
you're shrinking.
You start to disappear.
And no one seems to notice
No one seems to care.

But in our minds,
we're still just girls
Dancing through
the night.
There's so much more
to live for
Old souls with
futures bright!

Get Up and Move

Time to get up!

Get out of that chair!

Shake those old bones

but do it with care.

We don't want an incident, no EMTs.

Shake it all out,

but not too fast, please.

Twist and shout and do the Watusi.
Move those old joints
and get loosey-goosey.

Things are a-jiggling;
loose flesh a-wiggling,
And I just can't stop myself from a-giggling.

A silly dance is just what I needed.
I'm glad you could join me;
expectations exceeded.

We've got to keep moving.

It's move it or lose it.

And I think you still got it,

so don't ever quit.

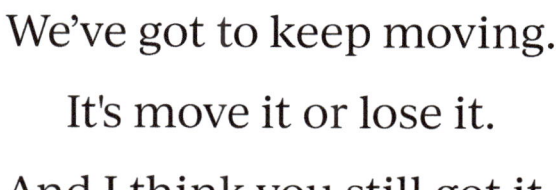

Moving

and

grooving

and making

life fun.

We're old,

but we're awesome

and so far from done!

Maggie Keefe

Maggie Keefe is the author of several silly, quirky children's books. Her latest undertaking, *Laugh Lines, Silly Poems for Seniors*, attempts to bring a smile to mature faces because why should kids have all the fun?

Maggie lives in the northeast kingdom of Vermont for half the year, escaping to Sarasota, Florida, when the long, cold Vermont winter sets in. What could be better than spending summer in the mountains, winter at the beach, *and* writing silly stories and poems?

Vaughan Duck

Vaughan loves drawing pictures that make kids giggle.

His first attempt at illustrating a children's book, *The Ant Explorer*, was shortlisted for the Lothian Centenary Children's Book Award.

Without knowing it, kids around the world have grown up with Vaughan's pictures, because he has illustrated over 300 text books and early readers for educational publishers.

Before he became mega-famous, Vaughan designed toys (so much fun) and kids' lunch boxes and backpacks.

www.ingramcontent.com/pod-product-compliance
Lightning Source LLC
Chambersburg PA
CBHW040859120626
46551CB00001B/81